MAY 2017

Knead with Speed, Chef Mead!

Kelly Doudna

Consulting Editor, Diane Craig, M.A./Reading Specialist

Published by ABDO Publishing Company, 4940 Viking Drive, Edina, Minnesota 55435.

Printed in the United States.

Credits
Edited by: Pam Price
Curriculum Coordinator: Nancy Tuminelly
Cover and Interior Design and Production: Mighty Media
Photo and Illustration Credits: Digital Vision, Francis Hammond/PhotoAlto, Hemera, Image 100, Image Source, Tracy Kompelien, PhotoDisc, Photosphere

Library of Congress Cataloging-in-Publication Data

Doudna, Kelly, 1963-
    Knead with speed, Chef Mead! / Kelly Doudna.
       p. cm. -- (Rhyme time)
    ISBN 1-59197-799-1 (hardcover)
    ISBN 1-59197-905-6 (paperback)
    1. English language--Rhyme--Juvenile literature. I. Title. II. Rhyme time (ABDO Publishing Company)

PE1517.D684 2004
428.1'3--dc22
                                                                    2004047355

SandCastle™ books are created by a professional team of educators, reading specialists, and content developers around five essential components that include phonemic awareness, phonics, vocabulary, text comprehension, and fluency. All books are written, reviewed, and leveled for guided reading, early intervention reading, and Accelerated Reader® programs and designed for use in shared, guided, and independent reading and writing activities to support a balanced approach to literacy instruction.

Let Us Know

After reading the book, SandCastle would like you to tell us your stories about reading. What is your favorite page? Was there something hard that you needed help with? Share the ups and downs of learning to read. We want to hear from you! To get posted on the ABDO Publishing Company Web site, send us e-mail at:

sandcastle@abdopub.com

SandCastle Level: Fluent

Words that rhyme do not have to be spelled the same. These words rhyme with each other:

bead

skied

deed

speed

knead

steed

lead

succeed

read

weed

Grace likes to be helpful.

Every day she tries to do at least one good **deed**.

When Caitlin makes a necklace, she carefully chooses each **bead**.

Keith makes his new race car **speed** across the floor.

Dale and Rick help bake bread.
It is Dale's turn to knead the dough.

Willy loves to ride his trusty **steed**.

Gabrielle, Lara, and Katie are racing each other.

Katie is in the **lead**.

Elizabeth works hard in school so she will **succeed.**

In the library, Mr. Tipton's class finds good books to read.

Alyssa's grandma shows her the difference between a flower and a weed.

Joshua **skied** through the ring of balloons.

Knead with Speed, Chef Mead!

Chef Mead wanted to succeed.

He wanted to exceed his previous deed.

CONTEST
FOR CHEFS

HOW MUCH DOUGH
CAN YOU KNEAD
WITH SPEED?

WIN A FABULOUS
SKI VACATION!

So he entered a contest
to see who could knead
the most dough
with the greatest speed.

15

The prize was a trip
to where people skied.

16

Chef Mead thought to himself, "I must win, yes indeed!"

He decided to read and read.
The cookbooks guaranteed
that he could take the lead.

Chef Mead knew he would need
all of his speed to complete the deed.

19

At the end of the contest,
everyone agreed
that he did indeed succeed.

Chef Mead
was the one
who could knead
with speed!

WINNER
CHEF WITH
THE MOST
SPEED

Rhyming Riddle

What do you call the first dandelion in line?

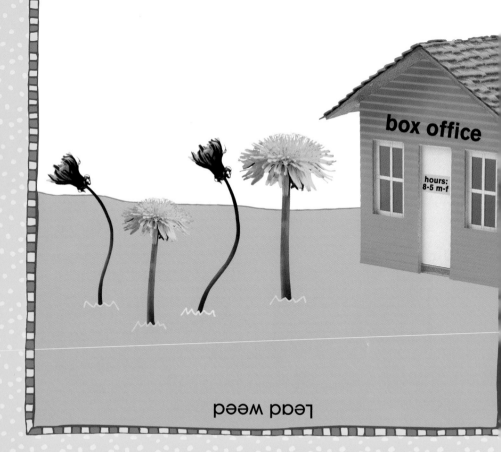

Lead weed

Glossary

deed. an act or action

exceed. to be more or better than expected

knead. to press, fold, and stretch something, such as bread dough

steed. a horse

weed. a plant that is growing where it shouldn't

About SandCastle™

A professional team of educators, reading specialists, and content developers created the SandCastle™ series to support young readers as they develop reading skills and strategies and increase their general knowledge. The SandCastle™ series has four levels that correspond to early literacy development in young children. The levels are provided to help teachers and parents select the appropriate books for young readers.

Emerging Readers
(no flags)

Beginning Readers
(1 flag)

Transitional Readers
(2 flags)

Fluent Readers
(3 flags)

These levels are meant only as a guide. All levels are subject to change.

To see a complete list of SandCastle™ books and other nonfiction titles from ABDO Publishing Company, visit www.abdopub.com or contact us at:
4940 Viking Drive, Edina, Minnesota 55435 • 1-800-800-1312 • fax: 1-952-831-1632